Arm Candy

BY

Hillary DePiano

Based on Pintosmalto (Pretty as a Picture) from The Tale of Tales by Giambattista Basile

Copyright 2017, 2025 Hillary DePiano
ALL RIGHTS RESERVED

ISBN: 978-1-944909-18-5 (paperback)
ISBN: 978-1-944909-19-2 (eBook)

For inquires, requests for permission, to secure rights for performance or other needs, please contact Hillary DePiano through her website at HillaryDePiano.com. **Discounted acting editions are available for schools and groups ordering in bulk for performance or classroom needs.**

CAUTION: Professional and amateurs are hereby warned that this play is fully protected under the copyright laws of the United States of America. All rights, including professional, amateur, motion pictures, recitation, lecturing, public reading, radio broadcasting, television, and the rights of translation into foreign languages are strictly reserved. In its present form, the play is dedicated to the reading public only.

The author controls all rights, including the amateur live stage performance rights,. The right of performance is not transferable.

Copying this play either in print or electronically without written permission of the author is strictly forbidden by law. No part of this publication may be reproduced, copied, stored in a retrieval system, transmitted in any form by any means, electronic, mechanical, photocopying, recording, performing, or otherwise, without written permission of the author.

Due authorship credit must be given on all programs, printing, and advertising for the play.

THE TALE OF TALES PROJECT

Giambattista Basile (1566–1632) wrote and compiled the 60 fairy tales within *The Pentamerone* (*Lo cunto de li cunti* in Neapolitan or *The Tale of Tales* in English) in Naples, Italy in the early 1600s. His sister, Adriana, published it in two volumes in 1634 and 1636 after his death. While not widely known, it's important historically because the Brothers Grimm later used it as the source for their far more famous fairy tale collection. *The Tale of Tales* contains the earliest known versions of fairy tales such as Sleeping Beauty, Cinderella, Rapunzel, Puss in Boots, Hansel and Gretel and more.

But I'm not interested in the stories everyone has heard of. I like the obscure ones, the weird ones lost to time. Why do we obsessively retell the same dozen fairy tales when there are plenty of other great ones we ignore?

It bothers me. So, since early 2013, I've been adapting these lesser-known tales for modern audiences to bring these stories back into circulation. I've modernized them with today's audiences in mind while still staying true to the spirit of the originals. Wherever possible, I also preserved the names from the original fairy tale and, where characters were unnamed, I've named them within the historical context and often with names from elsewhere in the Tales themselves.

This project is still ongoing. For the latest list of all the tales I've adapted from The Tale of Tales and what I'm working on next, visit HillaryDePiano.com.

BIBLIOGRAPHY

Basile, Giambattista (2007). Giambattista Basile's "The Tale of Tales, or Entertainment for Little Ones". Translated by Nancy L. Canepa, illustrated by Carmelo Lettere, foreword by Jack Zipes. Detroit, MI: Wayne State University Press. ISBN 978-0-8143-2866-8.

STANDALONE ONE-ACTS

There are standalone one-act versions of every fairy tale I've adapted from *The Tale of Tales*.

THE MYRTLE
35-45 minutes, 5 m 8 f (6-20+ performers possible)
A prince discovers his myrtle tree turns into a fairy maiden at sundown.

GOOSED!
(based on The Goose)
35-45 minutes, 2 m 6 f 8 any (11-20+ performers possible)
Two poor sisters rescue a golden goose but their sneaky neighbors want it for themselves.

ARM CANDY
(based on Pintosmalto)
45-60 minutes, 2 m, 4 f (5-7+ performers possible)
When a brilliant inventor builds the perfect husband out of sugar, he's stolen by a queen who wants him for herself.

THE FOURTH ORANGE
(based on The Merchant with characters from Carlo Gozzi's The Love of Three Oranges)
25-35 minutes, 4 m, 6 f, 5 any (7-20+ actors possible)
There were only supposed to be three oranges but Franceschina had to stick her nose where it didn't belong.

THE SHE BEAR
30-45 minutes, 2 m 2 f (4-10+ performers possible)
Is the prince losing his mind or has he really fallen in love with a bear?

VARDIELLO
10-15 minutes, 1 m, 1 f, 2 any
How much damage can one half-wit do before his mother gives him the boot? (Now published exclusively through Brooklyn Publishers!)

~

Want to combine plays to make an evening's entertainment?
You'll find shortened versions of the most popular fairy tales in this fun and fantastical full length!

THE FOURTH ORANGE
AND OTHER FAIRY TALES YOU'VE NEVER EVEN HEARD OF
100-120 minutes, 25w 12m 11any (11 to 60+ performers possible)
It's bedtime bedlam when a washed-up clown tries to sell three unruly princesses on something other than their fairy tale favorites.

Looking for something even more flexible?
Mix and match the tales above to create an evening's entertainment and I'll provide interstitial material and opening and closing scenes to connect the tales together no matter what combination you choose!

FOR MORE INFORMATION ABOUT THIS CUSTOM OPTION, EMAIL HILLARY DEPIANO AT HILLARY@HILLARYDEPIANO.COM.

ARM CANDY AT THE PRAIRIE SCHOOL IN WIND POINT, WISCONSIN

ARM CANDY

Arm Candy premiered on October 18, 2018 at The Prairie School in Wind Point, Wisconsin with the following cast and crew.

TRUFFALDINO	Audrey Braun
ANTONIELLO	Baxter Sohail
BETTA	Jasmine Roach
IGA	Natalie Dixon
PINTOSMALTO	Kyle Kane
QUEEN MENECA	Mia Stache
TOLLA	Kathrine Savas
SAMARITANA	Paris Liu

Director: Dena Roncone
Technical Director: Jake Bray

Set Designers/Crew Members
Abbas Bader, Wesley Eaton, Peter Vanko, Mitchell Warren

PRODUCTION NOTES

INCREASING OR DECREASING CAST SIZE

For smallest cast size, Tolla becomes Tollo so the performers playing Antoniello and Iga in the beginning can also play Tollo and Queen Meneca respectively. Need more roles? The marvels can be performers instead of props.

Please don't hesitate to contact me (hillary@hillarydepiano.com) for any reason. I'm here to help!

A NOTE ON TRANSLATION

Throughout this play, I have used the spelling of names and places from Giambattista Basile's work as translated by Nancy Canepa with one exception. While Canepa translates the name of the handmade man in Pretty as a Picture (presented here as Arm Candy) as Pinto Smauto, I have used the alternate spelling, Pintosmalto, because it is more widely known and commonly used.

CHARACTERS
(In order of appearance)

ANTONIELLO, merchant and Betta's father

BETTA, eccentric mechanicalchemist

IGA, Betta's former chambermaid, now assistant

PINTOSMALTO, handsome man Betta builds from sugar

QUEEN MENECA, Queen of Round Mountain

TOLLA, Queen Meneca's confident

SAMARITANA, old woman, blacksmith

SETTING
A fairytale kingdom.

TIME
The imaginary past.

ARM CANDY
SCENE 1

(The house of a merchant, Antoniello. Antoniello enters)

ANTONIELLO
Betta! I've just heard about the goldsmith boy. I don't understand why you've... Betta?

> *(The door to Betta's room bursts open, smoke billowing out. Her aesthetic is 17th century mad scientist. She wears improvised steampunk-esqu goggles and a work apron stained with grease and charred at the edges. She carries a fire bucket.)*

BETTA
It's alright, the fire is contained! Just a small calculation error, no need to—Oh, Papa! Perfect! You're just in time.

ANTONIELLO
Now, hold on a minute, we need to talk about--

BETTA
Sorry, Papa! Too much delay and BOOM, the compound ignites too early and we're all blown to bloody bits. Ha! No one could ever say the study of mechanicalchemy is boring! Here. For the shrapnel.

> *(She hands him a pair of the goggles. He struggles to figure out how they go on.)*

ANTONIELLO
The... the what?

> *(Betta whistles. A tea cart that she's modified with gears and alchemy rolls itself onto the stage. Atop it sits a singed and terrified Iga, Betta's assistant.)*

Is that your chambermaid?

IGA
(to herself)
This is fine. Completely fine. It's not the most terrifying experience of my life or anything.

BETTA
Hush, Iga, you're ruining the demonstration. Now, you'll have to picture it to scale, of course, with a proper seat and all your stock piled on but think of what we'd save on the donkeys alone!

ANTONIELLO
The cart moves on its own? Very impressive, my dear, though--

BETTA
Oh, that's not even near the best part. Iga!

IGA
Yes, mistress.

(Putting on a crude helmet. To herself.)
I hate my life.

(Bracing herself, she whistles. The cart picks up speed. She holds on for dear life as it really starts to go.)
Oh my gosh oh my gosh oh my gosh oh my gosh...

(Keeps repeating it to herself as the cart zooms off-stage)

BETTA
Ahahaha! Look at it go! See? We'd be halfway across the kingdom before the other merchants pulled on their boots. We could double our area. Triple it!

ANTONIELLO
I suppose but--

(The cart careens back in, too fast. A screaming Iga desperately tries to stay on.)

IGA
Aaaaaaaaaaaaaaaaaaaaaaaaaaaaaaaaaaaaaaaaaaah!

ANTONIELLO
Should it be smoking like that?

BETTA
Blast. Not again. Tuck and roll, Iga! Tuck and roll!

(The cart flies off stage. Betta and her father wince as it crashes and then, a moment later, explodes. A singed Iga totters in and collapses on the floor in a heap.)

IGA
I never thought I'd miss cleaning chamber pots.

ANTONIELLO
Betta...

BETTA
It's fine, Papa. I'm pretty sure that wall wasn't load bearing. But I really thought I had it this time. Oh, well, on to the next. Come on, quit your loafing, let's see what we can salvage.

(She tugs at Iga who doesn't budge.)

ANTONIELLO
Oh, my dearest Betta. What are you doing?

BETTA
I just said. It's a self driving cart or at least it will be once I can get it up to speed without it going all to pieces.

ANTONIELLO
I'm not talking about all your chemicals and clockwork. Do you ever think about the future?

BETTA
What do you mean? I'm building our future right here! All I ever do is try to invent ways to make our lives easier so maybe you'll finally sit back and let me handle--

ANTONIELLO
Nothing would be easier than if you just chose a husband!

BETTA
Not this again!

ANTONIELLO
I thought you liked the goldsmith boy, but you barely gave him a minute before you sent him away like all the others. He said you were as lovely as a jewel.

BETTA
I'll bet he did. A man who twists perfectly good metal into a useless bauble for his wrist just because he likes how it looks wants a wife that's much the same.

ANTONIELLO
I am only thinking of you, child! Look at me. I won't live forever. I can't bear to think of you all alone.

BETTA
Oh, Papa.

ANTONIELLO
Your life is bound to be filled with cold nights if you're only married to your work.

BETTA
For heaven's sake, I'm not married to my... Oh! That's it! It's so simple. Why didn't I think of it before?

ANTONIELLO
What? What is it?

(Betta hauls Iga to her feet)

BETTA
Come, you silly girl, there's work to be done!

IGA
No no no, can't you leave me to die in peace?

(Betta shoves Iga into her room)

BETTA
Hush. In you go. Start a list. We'll need supplies! Gem stones, sugar, almond paste... A perfect solution, really. Should have done it ages ago.

(Betta exits, mumbling to herself. Bewildered, her father calls after her)

ANTONIELLO
Betta?

(Betta pops back in)

BETTA
Papa, give the order. The preparations must begin right away. We'll have the feast within a fortnight!

ANTONIELLO
A feast? For what?

BETTA
My wedding, of course!

ANTONIELLO
You're getting married? To who? Didn't you just...

(She's gone)
I never know what's going on around here.

(exit)

SCENE 2

(Betta's room / workshop. There are tools, vials of mysterious chemicals and bits of inventions everywhere. Betta and Iga put the finishing touches on the figure lying on her work table.)

BETTA
Scalpel.

IGA
Scalpel, mistress.

BETTA
Sapphires.

IGA
Sapphires, mistress.

BETTA
Rubies.

IGA
Rubies, mistress.

BETTA
Pearls.

IGA
Pearls, mistress.

(Betta assembles the face.)

BETTA
Eyes of sapphires, lips of rubies, two neat rows of pearls for teeth. And, mmm, smell that? That's the dough. Half a qunintal of Palermo sugar and the same of almond paste with five flasks of rose water and cologne to keep him sweet. Then every ripping muscle and fine feature molded by hand with this silver scalpel. And if I can just coax this spun gold into a curl... there!

(Having arranged the spun gold into her creation's hair, she steps back to admire her handiwork.)
There. What do you say, Iga? Is he not the most beautiful man you've ever seen? And he smells good enough to eat!

IGA
Yes, mistress. But you are sure--

(Thunder. A storm begins outside)

BETTA

Ah, the storm! There's no time to lose! To your position! Secure the rods!

> *(Betta and Iga suit up in protective gear and secure a crude lightning rod to the outside of the windows. Betta attaches wires to the figure on the table as Iga slowly cranks a wheel. Outside, the storm rages. Lighting flashes. The body on the table twitches as the current courses through it. Betta pulls a large lever. Think 17th Century steampunk-esque Frankenstein.)*

It's working! We need more! Faster!

IGA

Yes, mistress! Faster! Faster!

> *(She turns the wheel faster and now the body is really moving, groaning and straining against its restraints.)*

BETTA

Aha! Yes! It's moving! It's alive. It's alive! IT'S ALIVE!

> *(She cackles maniacally.)*

We've done it, Iga! It lives!

> *(The figure, now Pintosmalto, slowly rises from the table.)*

IGA

In the name of the gods!

BETTA

Shh! It speaks!

PINTOSMALTO

Lady. Pretty lady.

BETTA

Oh, aren't you a dear. I shall call you Pintosmalto for you're as pretty as a picture.

PINTOSMALTO

Pintosmalto.

(He climbs down from the table and takes a few stiff legged steps towards them, arms outstretched. Iga recoils.)

BETTA

Keep hold of your senses, girl. Have you no faith in your mistress? Why do you think I crafted him from sugar? He's as gentle as a kitten. Aren't you, sweetie?

PINTOSMALTO

Nice Lady.

(He gives her an awkward stiff armed hug. Iga flees, screaming. She collides with Antoniello as he runs in.)

ANTONIELLO

Iga? Betta! Is everything alright? I heard screaming!

BETTA

Everything is wonderful, Papa! You're just in time! There's someone I'd like you to meet. Pintosmalto, this is my father, Antoniello.

PINTOSMALTO

Nice Lady's Papa. Nice Papa.

(Pats Antoniello on the head)

ANTONIELLO

Um, yes, well, it's nice to uh... Oh!

(Offers his hand to shake. Pintosmalto grabs it and shakes so vigorously Antoniello nearly falls over.)

Betta? What is the meaning of this? Who is this unusual man?

BETTA

Pintosmalto is my fiancé! I've chosen a husband at last, just as you always wished!

PINTOSMALTO

Yay!

ANTONIELLO

I see. Do I want to know where he came from?

BETTA

Probably not. Iga, you get the rod and I'll-- Iga? Where has that girl gone off to?

PINTOSMALTO

Pinto help! Is rod?

(He yanks the crank off the wall)

BETTA

Nuh-uh-uh. No touching Nice Lady's things!

(She takes the crank from him)

ANTONIELLO

My girl, are you quite sure about this?

BETTA

My calculations--

(Pinto has figured out which one is the rod. He hesitates before touching.)

PINTOSMALTO

Pinto help?

(Betta does it herself.)

BETTA

Pinto can help by just standing there and giving Nice Lady something handsome to look at. Don't you worry your pretty little head about any of this.

(She twists some wire into a flower shape and hands it to him)

PINTOSMALTO

Oh. Okay. Pinto just stand here with pretty head. Pinto stay out Nice Lady's way.

(He tucks the wire flower behind his ear and grins at her.)

BETTA

You see? He's perfect. I'm in love, Papa.

ANTONIELLO

Well, I suppose that's all there is to it. Come, lad. We'll have you fit for some proper clothes. The wedding day will be here before we know it.

(all exit)

SCENE 3

(Antoniello and Betta's home, decorated for Betta's wedding. Sounds of dancing offstage. The glamorous Queen Meneca and her confidant, Tolla, confer in secret.)

TOLLA

So little Betta is married at last. Not a bad turnout. Must have come from all along her father's trade route.

QUEEN MENECA

With the muddy road all over their boots to prove it. Disgusting. Commoners and their dusty little lives. My dear Tolla, how I long for the gleam of my own court.

TOLLA

Then we should take our leave, Queen Meneca.

QUEEN MENECA

Nonsense. I came all this way. I refuse to return empty bedded. After years with that withered old husk of a husband, don't I deserve a little arm candy?

TOLLA

You can't make a meal of sugar alone. But what does it matter what I think? Your heart is already set.

QUEEN MENECA

Ha! You know perfectly well I haven't had one of those in years! But if I did still have a heart, it would be set indeed. Such beautiful features! I must have him.

TOLLA

And the wife he acquired mere hours ago? The one whose wedding you're currently attending?

QUEEN MENECA

A minor detail. I will not leave an Adonis like that saddled to that greasy old kook of a merchant's daughter. Hush. He's coming and alone for once. Now is my chance. See that the carriage is ready to leave at a moment's notice.

TOLLA

As you wish. Happy hunting, my queen!

(Tolla exits. Pintosmalto enters dressed for the wedding, wearing the wire flower still tucked behind his ear. He executes an awkward bow.)

PINTOSMALTO

Hello, Fancy Lady. Nice hat.

QUEEN MENECA

What...

(Realizes he means her crown)
Ah.

PINTOSMALTO
So shiny!

QUEEN MENECA
...yes.

(to herself)
He's barely a quarter wit! This will be even easier than I thought!

PINTOSMALTO
Is late, Fancy Lady. Nice Lady say Pinto show guests to room.

QUEEN MENECA
Why, yes, that would be perfect! My room is in my castle back at Round Mountain. Can you show me there?

PINTOSMALTO
Pinto can! Make Nice Lady proud!

QUEEN MENECA
Oh, I'm sure she'll be absolutely delighted.

(Unnoticed, she plucks the wire flower and tosses it on the ground. She takes his arm as they exit. From offstage.)
Now, Tolla! Go go go!

(Sounds of Meneca's carriage peeling out in a hurry. Betta enters, hearing the commotion)

BETTA
Husband! Pintosmalto? Where has he gotten off to?

(She finds the discarded flower.)
He's gone? Unacceptable.

(She starts after the carriage. Her father enters.)

ANTONIELLO

Betta, there are some people I'd like you to-- What is it? Where are you going?

BETTA

I go to collect what's mine.

ANTONIELLO

But--

(She's already gone. He pursues her.)
Betta? Wait! Child, no, don't go, I beg of you!

(Exit)

SCENE 4

(Weeks of hard travel later. Betta struggles against the snow and wind, her travelling cloak huddling against the cold.)

BETTA

Pintosmalto? Pintosmalto! Gods, how long has it been? Days, weeks, months of searching with no provisions save my wits. And now hunger threatens to take even those from me. S-so cold... If only I could rest for... No. To stop here would be death. I must... I m-must...

(She falls from sheer exhaustion. With the last of her strength, she lights a beacon that projects a burst of fantastical colors. An old blacksmith woman, Samaritana, comes to investigate the beacon and discovers Betta, barely conscious. She pulls Betta to her feet, grabs the beacon and guides her to her shop. Betta defrosts by the fire, blinking her way back to consciousness)

Where am I? It was so cold, ice down to my bones, and I tried to hold on but then everything went black. But here is warmth, at last!

And a savior. Stranger, I would be dead now if you hadn't come to my aid. How can I ever repay you?

(Samaritana gives Betta a steaming mug)

SAMARITANA
Hush. Take the help. Here. Drink this.

(Betta drinks)
Now. Out with it. What's your story? No one travels alone in country such as this but the desperate or the senseless. I'd know which you are.

BETTA
My journey has been far longer than my tale. My husband is missing. I must find him and bring him home.

SAMARITANA
Never saw the use for a husband myself but only a fool would risk death chasing a man who can lose himself like a sock.

BETTA
I am not a fool. At the start, yes, I was full of the principle of the thing, thinking only that I had been stolen from. But I'd have turned back months ago were it not for more recent complications.

(She removes her cloak to reveal that she is heavily pregnant.)

SAMARITANA
Gods' teeth. You're with child.

BETTA
Such a blasted inconvenience! Now I'll be ruined by gossips if I return without my husband. My father is old enough, the shock could kill him!

SAMARITANA
And you think to find your man in this harsh country?

BETTA
There is nowhere left to search! But I fear I've risked everything

for another dead end. The last name on my father's route is a great Queen.

SAMARITANA

Ha! Queen Meneca is only great the way you'd call a plague so. She's as shallow as a dish with as much feeling as hunk of cold iron. Now that you say it, she did come home a few months ago with a dazzling man, eyes like gems, cheekbones like they were carved from marble.

BETTA

That's my Pintosmalto! It must be. Thank the gods, I've found him at last! Please, take me to him at once.

SAMARITANA

Oh, lass. You're too late. He's forgotten you. She's married him herself.

BETTA

No. I will not accept it. I only need a moment with him, and he'll return to me at once, I'm certain of it.

SAMARITANA

Very well. But she keeps the man as she does all her beautiful things: Locked away for no eyes but her own. They say she's got quite a collection of treasures. She'd go mad for this lantern of yours.

BETTA

My emergency beacon? But it's just a simple chemical reaction.

SAMARITANA

She wouldn't care about anything other than it's pretty and no one else has anything like it. Meneca knows nothing of manipulating materials. Just people.

BETTA

Hmm. You put me in mind of a plan.

SAMARITANA

Then count me in. I have no love for Queen Meneca. If your

happiness comes at her misery, I'm happy to lend my forge to that service.

(They shake on it and confer as the scene fades to black)

SCENE 5

(Queen Meneca's castle. Queen Meneca paces. Outside the window, Betta's beacon puts on a colorful show.)

QUEEN MENECA
Look at those lights, the way they dance upon the stones! And a whole crowd of filthy peasants down there gobbling up the sight when such beauty should belong to me alone. Ah, finally. Here comes Tolla with my prize.

(Tolla leads two strangers-- Betta and Samaritana in disguise.)

TOLLA
I found the tinkers, your majesty, but they have refused to sell.

QUEEN MENECA
What do you mean I can't buy it? No one has a treasure store like I do!

BETTA
(disguising her voice)
I care nothing for your gold. I travel in search of wonders. I have seen trinkets and treasures like yours all over the world. Even the finest item in your collection is nothing I haven't already seen.

QUEEN MENECA
Ah, but the loveliest thing I possess is not made of silver or gold. It is a man.

BETTA
Is that so? I would like to see such a creature. Speak with him. Perhaps we can arrange a trade.

QUEEN MENECA

Perhaps we can. It would, of course, be unseemly to leave a stranger alone with the queen's husband for a night, but perhaps with a door between you, a keyhole for talk and observation. Would you trade your lantern for an evening outside Pintosmalto's bedchamber?

BETTA

Yes, that seems satisfactory. We shall go fetch our device and settle the trade at once.

(aside to Samaritana)

She took the bait! This will be easier than I thought! A few whispers through the keyhole and Pintosmalto will break down the door to get to me. We'll be on our way back home before daybreak!

SAMARITANA

Be careful, Betta. The easy fixes rarely keep. You're clever, but so is she, in her own way.

(Betta and Samaritana exit)

TOLLA

So, my queen, do you think wine will be enough to take care of him or should I fetch some of your powders?

QUEEN MENECA

Why not both? Pintosmalto!

TOLLA

I do like how you think.

(Tolla exits. Pintosmalto enters, dressed like a king)

There you are husband. These fine clothes do suit you. I never tire of looking at your handsome figure.

PINTOSMALTO

Pinto's butt itches.

QUEEN MENECA
But then you always go and spoil it by opening your mouth.

(Tolla has returned with the wine and powders. Queen Meneca mixes a pinch into the glass and hands it to him)

Here. Drink this and then get yourself to bed.

PINTOSMALTO
Uh, OK.

(He does so and immediately gets drowsy.)

Pinto so tired...

TOLLA
Perfect. I'll go get the girl.

(Tolla exits. Pintosmalto yawns. Queen Meneca shoves him into his bedchamber and locks the door. Tolla returns with Betta and the beacon.)

TOLLA
As promised, here is the door to Pintosmalto's chambers.

BETTA
Let me see this keyhole. Ah, there is he. Yes. This will do. As agreed.

(She hands over the beacon.)

QUEEN MENECA
Then you have until the sun rises. Come, Tolla!

(As soon as Queen Meneca and Tolla exit, Betta runs to the keyhole and whispers through it.)

BETTA
Pintosmalto, it's Betta. If you knew the trials I've undergone to find you but there's no time. We've got to get out of here so smash down this door before-- Pintosmalto? Pst! Hey! Husband! Don't

just lie there on your back like a dead thing. Turn towards me at least so I can see your face. Hello? Are you even listening? Why in heaven won't you look at me?

> *(All through the night, she tries to wake him to no avail. She's still banging on the door and calling out for him as the sun rises and Queen Meneca enters)*

Pintosmalto. Pintosmalto! Please, please listen to me! The night is nearly spent. I have shouted myself hoarse for hours, beaten my fists raw and still you haven't approached or spoken or shown any sign of listening at all. Is your heart really so cold?

QUEEN MENECA

The sun has risen. Your time is up. I trust your reward was everything you hoped it would be.

BETTA

What? No! This is an outrage! He never even---

QUEEN MENECA

Oh, dear. You aren't going to prove troublesome, are you? I'd hate to have my guards make an example of you in the square.

> *(Betta slips back into her disguised voice)*

BETTA

Ah, no. No trouble here, majesty. I will go.

> *(to herself)*

But I will be back. With a treasure that makes that beacon look like a chamber pot.

> *(Betta exits.)*

SCENE 6

> *(Queen Meneca's castle, several days later. She and Tolla are trying to play a game, but Pintosmalto keeps getting in their way.)*

TOLLA
It's your turn, my queen.

QUEEN MENECA
I know but-- Will you go away? How can I concentrate with you at my elbow the whole time?

PINTOSMALTO
Pinto want learn game. What this one for? Oops!

(He pokes at a piece, spilling the game everywhere)

QUEEN MENECA
You absolute imbecile! Can't we at least have one evening's amusements without you bumbling all-- Oh!

(A beautiful tinkling melody begins outside. Pintosmalto, Queen Meneca and Tolla are immediately entranced.)

TOLLA
What is that? What is making that lovely melody?

(Tolla exits)

PINTOSMALTO
Pretty music! Make Pinto feel free.

(He absentmindedly takes a flower from a vase and tucks it behind his ear)

QUEEN MENECA
What are you still doing here, Pintosmalto? Go up to my chambers and wait there until I have need of you.

PINTOSMALTO
But Pinto like pretty music.

(She rips the flower from his ear and crushes it. Outside, the music stops.)

QUEEN MENECA
Pinto does what he is told. Pinto goes to my chambers and stays there until I call for him. I swear, you grow dumber by the day. Now, go!

PINTOSMALTO
Pinto go.

> *(Pintosmalto exits as Tolla leads Betta and Samaritana in, wearing new disguises. They wheel in a covered bird cage.)*

TOLLA
Queen Meneca, these minstrels have come to present you with their musical marvel.

QUEEN MENECA
Minstrels? Then where are their instruments?

> *(Betta pulls off the cover to reveal a gilded cage covered in bells. Meneca gasps as the bells chime an enchanted melody.)*

QUEEN MENECA
What magic is this? No royal in the land has anything half so wonderful. They'll all writhe with envy. I must have it! Name your price!

BETTA
I want no price but to meet alone with Pintosmalto.

QUEEN MENECA
You again. I should have known. After your insolence? I don't care how exquisite it is, I refuse.

> *(Samaritana cranks a key on the cage. A jeweled bird rises up and dances to the music.)*

QUEEN MENECA
That's quite remarkable, and the way the feathers shine is truly

enchanting... but, still, I shouldn't-- Oh!

(The bird begins to sing)

TOLLA
Be strong, majesty.

QUEEN MENECA
Yes. You're right. I must...

(More mechanical birds join the song. The inside of the cage lights like a concert. Queen Meneca can hardly contain herself.)

TOLLA
Deep breaths. Resist.

BETTA
Come! Let's take our work to someone with more discerning taste. No one here has the refinement to appreciate its artistry and delicate workings.

(They start to pull it away. Queen Meneca whimpers. Tolla holds her back.)

SAMARITANA
Ah, yes. But first, we'll play it in the square, let every last peasant get up close and really enjoy it.

(Queen Meneca lunges in front of them)

QUEEN MENECA
No! Wait! You can have your time alone with Pintosmalto. I swear it! Tonight. You can wait outside his bedchamber again and--

BETTA
So you can stuff his ears with cotton or whatever treachery you worked last time? No. I will meet him here and now, no doors between us.

TOLLA
You dare to order Queen Meneca around like a common--

(Betta gives Samaritana a signal and they start moving again)

QUEEN MENECA

Fine! You may have your meeting, exactly as you said. Just get my beautiful birds safely into my treasure room, and I'll send for Pintosmalto.

(Betta and Samaritana exit with cage.)
Pintosmalto! Come down here at once!

TOLLA

But, my queen, unchaperoned, not even a door to--

QUEEN MENECA

We'll repeat our trick; pay the fare in bad coin. What's the harm to us?

TOLLA

None, I suppose. I'll prepare the wine.

(Tolla exits as Pintosmalto enters)

PINTOSMALTO

Pinto come cause Fancy Lady--

QUEEN MENECA

Do shut your mouth. I'm in no mood for your prattle.

PINTOSMALTO

Oh. Okay. Pinto shut mouth.

(Tolla returns with the wine)

QUEEN MENECA

Thank you, Tolla. You. Down this.

PINTOSMALTO

But wine make Pinto sleepy. Give Pinto weird dreams.

QUEEN MENECA

You dare argue with me? After all I've done for you? Tolla and I could be having a peaceful evening right now if I hadn't taken you and your endless idiotic yammering into our home. Do as I say! Drink it. Now.

PINTOSMALTO
Pinto drink.

(Pintosmalto drinks the wine and sits. He's already drooping as Betta enters.)

QUEEN MENECA
Just in time. We'll leave you to your reward.

(Queen Meneca and Tolla exit. Betta runs to Pintosmalto, asleep with his eyes open.)

BETTA
Ah, Pintosmalto! They'll be no ignoring me this time! Now, look at me and remember who I am. It's me, your true wife. That witch stole you and now we've got to... Hello? Why do you stare like that? Has it been so long that you don't recognize your Betta? Or do you pretend to ignore me? This is no time for sulks, you hopeless man, I'm carrying your child and we'll all face ruin unless--

(Pintosmalto snores, his eyes closing. The sleeping draught in the wine has knocked him out completely.)

Asleep? Are you so unmoved by my plight you cannot even stay awake to hear it? Does my suffering truly bore you that much? Wake up! You sleep but it's me trapped in this nightmare!

(Queen Meneca enters as Betta tries to shake him awake.)

QUEEN MENECA
What's this? Get your hands off my property.

BETTA
I was trying to wake him. He's been asleep the whole time.

QUEEN MENECA
You should thank me. He's not much for conversation anyway. Poor dear must have been all worn out. I do put him to good use every night.

BETTA
How dare you! I'll have your neck, you--

(Betta lunges for her, but Samaritana rushes in and hold her back)

SAMARITANA
Stop it! Have you taken leave of your senses?

BETTA
Fine. But the next time--

QUEEN MENECA
As if I'd ever let you in my doors again now that I see your true colors. You've gotten your payment. Now get your bloated body out of my castle before I have you tossed out.

BETTA
Why you--

SAMARITANA
Shh! Patience, Betta.

(leading her out of the castle)

BETTA
We don't have time for patience! The baby is coming! It will emerge any day now and Papa and I's lives will be ruined. We'll build something else, try again.

SAMARITANA
She's playing you for a fool and she'll only do it again! Be sensible. Only a dolt does the same thing over and over expecting a different result. We'll go back to the forge, make a new plan--

BETTA
A dolt, am I? Fine. I don't need your help, anyway.

SAMARITANA
Now, Betta, don't--

BETTA
I don't need anyone! I'll handle this myself.

(She storms away.)

SCENE 7

(Queen Meneca's castle, several days later. Betta bursts in, pursued by Tolla.)

TOLLA
I couldn't stop her. She just barreled through the door! I'll call the guards, have them--

QUEEN MENECA
Not yet. Have you brought me another present, silly girl? I do so enjoy watching you waste these treasures on hopeless chances.

BETTA
I have no patience for chatter. Let's get down to it.

(Betta whistles and an ornate cart set for tea wheels itself in. She whistles again and the cart dances, spinning around the room in lovely patterns, until it finally stops in front of Queen Meneca. Mechanical hands rise up from the cart and serve her tea and tiny sandwiches.)

There. Now, do you want it or not?

QUEEN MENECA
(nibbling a sandwich)
Hmm, yes. I believe I do.

BETTA
Good, this time I want--

QUEEN MENECA
No. I am done playing games, merchant girl.

(Betta abandons her disguise)

BETTA
So you admit it! You stole my husband!

QUEEN MENECA
I stole nothing.

TOLLA
It's true. The man came of his own free will.

BETTA
You lie! Bring him here. Let me talk to him. If I had but an hour alone with Pintosmalto, he'd be mine again.

QUEEN MENECA
Is that so? What would you stake on it?

BETTA
I've already shown you the cart.

QUEEN MENECA
No. This time I name the price. The cart and you. You to stay here in my palace as my slave, making me treasures like this every day. And when the child is born, you give it to me and go along when I say it is mine. I have no love for children, but they are profitable enough when you call them heirs marry them off nice and young.

TOLLA
Meneca--

BETTA
Fine. I accept. It doesn't matter what the price is for failure when success is guaranteed.

QUEEN MENECA
Wonderful! Then let us waste no time in settling our little wager. Pintosmalto! Come down here! Tolla, go and fetch my husband a drink. I'm sure they'll have much to discuss, and I'd hate for his

throat to be too parched for conversation.

(Betta misses the obvious wink Meneca gives Tolla)

TOLLA

As you wish.

(Pintosmalto enters.)

QUEEN MENECA

There are you, Pintosmalto. What's this?

(He's twisted some wire into a crude flower and tucked it behind his ear)

A bit of twisted metal. Trash.

(She tosses it.)

There. Much better. Such a handsome figure. You're lucky I don't keep you locked up with the rest of my treasures.

PINTOSMALTO

Pinto lucky.

QUEEN MENECA

You see? I've never chained you, never made you stay.

PINTOSMALTO

Where Pinto go?

QUEEN MENECA

Exactly. There's nowhere else you'd rather be.

(Tolla returns with the wine)

But better to protect what's mine all the same. Sit. Drink this. And I don't want to hear any protests this... Oh.

(He's already downed it and plopped into the chair. He yawns as Betta returns.)

BETTA

Pintosmalto! Finally! Tell this woman that I...

(He snores, apparently dead asleep)
Pintosmalto? Asleep again? It's barely noon. How can this be?

(She sees the cup)
The wine! I should have known. You've been drugging him!

(Queen Meneca laughs)

QUEEN MENECA
What's the matter, girl? Finding it harder than you thought to win the man back? I wonder what lovely trinket my clever little captive will make me first.

BETTA
Villain! You cheated!

QUEEN MENECA
You may cry all about it to my guards. They'll be along as soon as your hour is up to drag you to my dungeons. But gently, of course, to protect my investment. I'm already thinking of several profitable options for that little brat just as soon as you pop it out for me.

BETTA
You will never lay a hand on my child, nor will I make you anything!

QUEEN MENECA
Then you can have your baby in the stocks and let the cold take you both for all I care.

(She storms out)

BETTA
Oh, Pintosmalto! I've really done it this time. I should have listened to my friend, should have checked my foolish pride, should have made myself a husband with a face like a normal man instead of a god and Meneca never would have... All those suitors that only wanted me to be something sweet and pretty on their arm and I wanted to show them. I wanted them to see that I... But then, I only did the same thing to you they'd have done to me. I am a fool.

PINTOSMALTO

No. Pinto not remember all but he remember Nice Lady not fool. Nice Lady smart. The most smart.

BETTA

You're awake? But how can this be?

PINTOSMALTO

Two time wine make Pinto dream of Nice Lady. But Nice Lady sad and Pinto not hear what she say. So Pinto think like sneaky queen and switch sleepy powder with flour. Make bad wine taste. But Pinto stay awake!

BETTA

Amazing!

PINTOSMALTO

Pinto not fool either, only new. But understand now that everything not sugar and almond paste.

BETTA

Oh, Pintosmalto. I'm so sorry.

PINTOSMALTO

No. Pinto sorry. He cause Nice Lady lot of trouble. Memory from start all wiggly. He not know how to find Nice Lady so he stay. Stay was bad.

BETTA

Then we leave now and we start over. All three of us.

PINTOSMALTO

Nice Lady got somebody hiding in there?

BETTA

Yes, actually. A baby. Our baby. You're going to be a papa!

PINTOSMALTO

Oh! Pinto not even know how that work but he learn! Pinto be best papa ever!

BETTA
I have no doubt you will be. But we've no time to waste. We've got to get out of here.

PINTOSMALTO
But how? Fancy Lady got guards with pointy sticks! Horses run faster than Pinto!

(Betta strips the tea setting and lacy tablecloth off the cart to reveal the gears and other workings below. She sets to work on it with the help of the hands that served the tea.)

BETTA
This thing can outrun any horse if I can just get it up to full speed. But it's not working right.

PINTOSMALTO
What this part do?

(He leans in too close)

BETTA
Stay out of--

(catches herself)
Not quite so close, alright? That's the gear for the front wheels. They pull the whole thing forward. But they're not giving me enough power.

PINTOSMALTO
And what these pretty little wheels back here do?

BETTA
Nothing. Those are just decorative.

PINTOSMALTO
Oh. But could they maybe also help?

(She looks at him, then the wheels)

BETTA
Why, yes, I do believe they could. I could rig it in half a minute if I just had some wire. Where is that... Aha!

(She produces the original wire flower)
Hm. Not quite enough. I kept this for you. When I thought you had forgotten me, I hoped it would--

(Pinto retrieves the metal flower he made from where Meneca tossed it earlier)

PINTOSMALTO
Pinto never forget Nice Lady. Pinto feel her fingerprints pressed into his heart.

(He shows her his flower. They have a moment. Then both untwist the flowers and get to work wiring up the back wheels.)

BETTA
It goes around just like this. Make sure you tighten the-- perfect! You're a natural! Iga will be so relieved to be back scrubbing chamber pots. Now, give it a spin. Ha! Wonderful! This might actually work!

(As they work, Queen Meneca and Tolla burst in, mid conversation)

QUEEN MENECA
I still don't think he has the wits for it. But alert the guards anyway, have them block every exit.

TOLLA
I tried to as soon as I checked the powders but I could find no sign of-- There!

(They spot Betta and Pintosmalto)

BETTA
Meneca!

QUEEN MENECA
Well. I see you've played quite a trick on me, husband. Though it won't do you any good. I don't care how clever that girl is, she can't use potions and bits of gears to make a way out. You're trapped!

(She screams as the wall behind them explodes. Samaritana bursts through the ruined wall.)

SAMARITANA
Shows what you know! Nothing easier to make than a hole!

(Queen Meneca and Tolla struggle to right themselves from the debris)

TOLLA
What is the meaning of this?

QUEEN MENECA
My castle!

BETTA
Samaritana! You came for me? I thought--

SAMARITANA
What? That I wasn't young once, didn't think I could hold the whole world up with nothing but my own two hands? I've done it both ways, Betta, and life's better when you've got somebody to help you clean up your mess. Speaking of, you weren't fooling! Those things really do go right to pieces when you try to get em up to speed!

BETTA
Actually, we may have fixed that particular design flaw. Just a few more adjustments and we'll all be on our way. Hop on!

SAMARITANA
Alright, but I got a fair bit of luggage.

(With effort, she drags in a huge sack of treasure which includes the bird cage and

beacon Betta traded earlier)

QUEEN MENECA
My treasures! Thieves! Guards! Tolla, do something!

SAMARITANA
Your guards are going to be a bit held up what with all the doors being welded shut and all.

TOLLA
We had an agreement! Besides, you didn't make all of that! There's a fortune in gold there.

SAMARITANA
That's for our trouble. Parts and labor.

(Betta and Pintosmalto finish the cart repairs)

BETTA
Got it! Now, all we need to do is add the compound and cross our fingers that the whole thing doesn't blow.

(She rubs the compound on the new wires)

PINTOSMALTO
No go boom, nice cart. Pinto rather zoom!

BETTA
So far so good! Everybody on! It's time to go home.

(Betta and Samaritana get onto the cart. Pintosmalto starts to get on after them.)

QUEEN MENECA
And where exactly do you think you're going, husband?

BETTA
Stop calling him that! Your marriage was a sham.

QUEEN MENECA
No, you foolish girl! Mine is the real one. A Queen's word is worth

triple the one of a nothing like you. He is and will always be my husband because I say so.

BETTA
That is not how it--

PINTOSMALTO
Pinto Fancy Lady's actual husband? Is real marriage?

BETTA
Pintosmalto, sweetie, no, she--

QUEEN MENECA
Yes. I say that you are bound to me, and it is so. There is nothing that girl can do to change that.

PINTOSMALTO
Pinto see. Then if Pinto Fancy Lady's real husband, that make Pinto King. So treasure is Pinto's.

(Samaritana is struggling to get the last sack of treasure on the cart. Pintosmalto lifts it on with one hand as if it weighs nothing)

QUEEN MENECA
Now, wait just a minute...

TOLLA
Oh brother.

PINTOSMALTO
So King Pinto take all this and go. And if Fancy Lady bother us ever again, King Pinto come back for rest. Maybe take castle too. Kick Fancy Lady out, make Nice Lady Queen. Kings can do stuff like that, nobody say boo. Or maybe Pinto not need tell anyone he King. Maybe Pinto just take this stuff, go with Nice Lady, forget all about King thing. Fancy Lady can pick.

QUEEN MENECA
But you... I'm the one that... Curses.

TOLLA
I can't believe we've been thwarted by a guy who can barely conjugate a verb.

BETTA
Pintosmalto, that was amazing!

SAMARITANA
I'm starting to see why this fella of yours was worth all the trouble.

BETTA
(she has a contraction)
Argh! Come on, everyone. Baby says it's time to go!

(Pintosmalto jumps onto the cart. Betta whistles and the cart rockets forward. They zoom out the hole in the wall)

TOLLA
This isn't over yet! I'll free the guards. We can--

QUEEN MENECA
Oh, Tolla, leave it. Let them go.

TOLLA
But they stole from you! Your treasures! Your husband!

QUEEN MENECA
A cheater can hardly complain if she's cheated. Next time I want to decorate my arm, tell me to get a bangle. Come, old friend. We can have an evening in peace for the first time in ages, just you and I.

TOLLA
Now that would indeed be a beautiful thing!

(They exit companionably)

SCENE 8

(Antoniello's house. Iga tends Antoniello,

who looks deathly ill.)

IGA
(squinting into the distance)
Is that... Mistress Betta?

(Antoniello sees them too. He tosses the blanket aside and jumps up and down, celebrating and hugging Iga, completely healthy again.)

ANTONIELLO
Betta? My child! Oh, Iga, she's returned to us at last!

(Betta, Pintosmalto and Samaritana zoom in on the cart.)

BETTA
(through labor pains)
Brake! Brake! I can't hold it any longer!

(She screams as Samaritana stops the cart so fast the baby shoots out of Betta and into Antoniello's arms. All celebrate and fuss over the new arrival.)

SCENE 9

(Antoniello and Betta's home, several months later. It is set up like a showroom, Betta's inventions lining the walls, showcasing the new family business. Antoniello enters carrying a box of more gadgets, calling to someone off-stage. Iga follows close behind.)

ANTONIELLO
Well, tell them to double the order then! Half the country is coming to tonight's demonstration and we want there to be feast

enough for everyone!

IGA
(tries to take the box from him)
Master, let me. You shouldn't be lifting so much at your age.

ANTONIELLO
Nonsense! Retirement agrees with me. Now that I have my Betta back, a grandchild for my knee, I'm as hearty as a lad again. With the thrill of this new family business, why, I feel I could take on the whole army of Round Mountain myself.

(Samaritana enters, part of the family now.)

SAMARITANA
Ha! Not likely, you old coot. Though I almost wish old Queen Meneca would try and start something, just to see us spending her gold with greasy fingers and sharing her treasures with everyone.

(Betta enters from her workshop, her goggles atop her head, her apron stained with grease. Pintosmalto follows behind in a similar state, with his own filthy work gear and the baby strapped to his chest.)

BETTA
She'd hate just about everything about this life we've all built here together.

PINTOSMALTO
It not always pretty.

(Pintosmalto pulls on his goggles.)
But pretty not everything.

(Betta pulls on her goggles.)

BETTA
Are you ready, my loves?

(Pintosmalto secures goggles on the baby.)

PINTOSMALTO

Ready!

(Pintosmalto and Betta pull a large switch together, plunging the stage into darkness.)

Sweet.

End of play

Also by Hillary DePiano

HillaryDePiano.com

Full Length Plays

The Love of Three Oranges
comedy / fantasy /commedia dell'arte
90 to 120 minutes, 8 f, 8 m, 5 any (13-40+ actors possible: 7-20 f, 5-20 m)
A prince is cursed to fall in love with three magical oranges.

The Green Bird
comedy / fantasy /commedia dell'arte
90 to 120 minutes, 4 m 6 f 3 any (13-40+ actors possible)
Four royals, two clowns, and way too many talking statues must unravel the mystery of the green bird before an evil queen destroys the kingdom.

The Servant of 123 Masters
comedy / fantasy /commedia dell'arte
60 minutes (11-12 actors possible)
a hilarious parody of Sesame Street by way of Carlo Goldoni's The Servant of Two Masters

The Montholouges
contemporary / comedy / drama
30 to 70 minutes, 1 m 1 f 14 any (1-16 actors possible)
A funny, touching monologue play about all the ways who we are intersects with when we are.

One Act Plays

Week Daze
comedy
45 to 60 minutes, 6-7 any
Week Daze zooms out and looks at our daily routines from a new perspective as all five weekdays play out simultaneously across the stage in a comic ballet.

The Love of Three Oranges (One Act Version)
comedy / fantasy /commedia dell'arte
35 to 40 minutes, 8 f, 6 m, 4 any (10-30+ actors possible)
A prince is cursed to fall in love with three magical oranges.

The Green Bird (One Act Version)
comedy / fantasy / commedia dell'arte
35 to 45 minutes, 4 m 6 f 3 any (12-40+ actors possible)
Four royals, two clowns, and way too many talking statues must unravel the mystery of the green bird before an evil queen destroys the kingdom.

Nana's Happy Happy Good News Only Birthday Video Chat
comedy / streaming / contemporary
30 to 40 minutes, 5 m, 5 f (7-10 performers possible, flexible genders)
When a storm ruins the family's plans, Nana's grandkids organize a birthday video chat! But can this group of disasters pretend they've got their act together, or will life have other plans?

Daddy Issues
drama
15 to 20 minutes, 1 female, 1 male, 3 any
A young woman must confront the ghost of her past.

Polar Twilight
comedy / holiday
20 to 25 minutes, 3 f, 3 m (6 actors possible: 0-5 f, 1-6 m)
Everything you know about Santa is wrong and the truth kind of... sucks. Vampire Santa Claus... but in a cute way!

New Year's Thieve
comedy / holiday
30 to 35 minutes, 2 m 3 f 3 any (7 to 10+ actors possible)
Someone's stolen the New Year and the main suspect is... Frosty the coat rack?

Short Plays (10-15 Minutes)

The Raven / Lenore

The Three Little Pigs and the Big Bad Storm

The (Completely Inaccurate) Legend of the Mummy Witch House

The Complete Novels of Jane Austen: Now New and Improved!

Three Padded Walls

Masks

Non-Fiction

Building a Writing Life
Do you want to write but have no idea where to begin? Building a Writing Life is the beginner writer's guide you've been looking for!

Make Ready to Write!
From novels and scripts to memoirs and more, your ultimate guide to prepping for a major writing project!

NaNo What Now?
Finding your editing process, revising your NaNoWriMo book and building a writing career through publishing and beyond.

~

Writing as T. W. Seller
TheWhineSeller.com
Sell Their Stuff
From eBay Trading Assistants to multichannel seller assistance, your ultimate guide to consignment selling online as a part-time income or full-time business

eBay Marketing Makeover
Increase sales and grow traffic to your eBay items by encouraging word of mouth, focusing on your ideal buyers, and optimizing your selling for search and mobile

Beyond Amazon, eBay, and Etsy
Free and low cost alternative marketplaces, shopping cart solutions and e-commerce storefronts

About the Author

Hillary DePiano is a playwright, fiction and non-fiction author best known for fantastically funny fairy tales, surprisingly sweet slapstick and unrelentingly upbeat writing advice. With over two dozen plays for everyone from pre-schoolers and up, she's been honored to have her work performed in schools and theatres around the world.

A consummate cheerleader for writers at every experience level, Hillary teaches a variety of workshops and writing classes on everything from storycraft to marketing and beyond. She also teaches eBay, e-commerce and selling online under the name T. W. Seller (TheWhineSeller.com).

For more information about her books, plays, and blogs or for the schedule of upcoming events and workshops, visit HillaryDePiano.com.

www.ingramcontent.com/pod-product-compliance
Lightning Source LLC
Chambersburg PA
CBHW061259040426
42444CB00010B/2426